REAL LIVES

REAL LIVES

ROGER BELL

To Bob

*For capturing
the aching beauty
of sun on father's
floor.*

Roger Bell

BLACK MOSS PRESS
1997

Published in October 1997 by Black Moss Press, 2450 Byng Road, Windsor, Ontario N8W 3E8. Black Moss Press books are distributed by Firefly Books, 3680 Victoria Park Ave., Willowdale, Ontario, M2H 3K1. All orders should be directed there.

Black Moss would like to acknowledge the support of the Department of Canadian Heritage and the Ontario Arts Council.

We would also like to acknowledge the support of the Canada Council for the Arts for our publishing program.

ISBN 0-88753-305-1

Acknowledgements

My thanks to the wonderful poet and friend, John Lee, for his wise counsel in the preparation of this book.

"Poet in hockey dressing room" appeared in a different form in Mythtakes (Midland: Whizzyfig Press, 1984) "Packing", "Small histories in the snow", and "The goaltender is missing" first appeared in That Sign of Perfection (Windsor: Black Moss Press, 1995)

Cover photograph is by Rob Gurdebeke, used with permission of *The Windsor Star*.

This book is for my parents;
would that they were here to read it.

Contents

WATCHING GRANDFATHER FALL

Putting summer into the attic
I'm up in the stale heat
with you below me
on the risk of a ladder
handing up last goodbyes
and the earth shrugs
and I see your eyes
frightened and white
your hand a plea,
I reach and apprehend only air,
you land on your wrist
snapping the ulna like a lapsed vow
leaving me outstretched
my hand mute   gaping.

Two years later in fall you die
only a handful of blocks away
from where I party and confuse my brain
with beer and noise and transient women;
you put things in their proper place
then lie down
on crisp white sheets
and sleep away;
won't the tilting world
let you wait a day
till I can be there
maybe pull you back
but no   you must go
once again leave me
shaking hands with emptiness.
 You helped me learn baseball
where now I play third base
and balls off the bat are launched
but I see them   mostly
and my glove knows
where to meet them,
how to hold them

7

squiggling like mad minnows;
still, there are times
when the ground shifts,
when earth and sky seem
not to mesh
when eye is not enough
when I wind up
extended, eating dirt,
feeling my gloved hand
flapping on air only,
seeing a whiteness
laugh by
into the green
and open
outfield

BAD HOP

"At least you kept it in the infield"

The redhaired bigboy at the plate
uncoils like slow thunder
his wrists roll as he
turns on one and
murders it down the line

the first white puff of lime
in evening air triggers you
unleash to the outside right
of your right foot swing across the left leg
your left arm brushing your ribs shoulder to chin
ninety degrees your wrist adjusts
your glove thumb splays away from the index
fingers all v'd stiff so the pocket maws
eyes on the ball   elbow locks
there, be true
for the second hop is in   isn't
that too bad
isn't that
just the way   you almost have time to reflect
 as it whims up off a stone
        cracks like split atom
        into your surprise
        your turbinate shocks sideways
        and your eyes unlock, see the ground rise until
        you're curldigging dirt for answers
        through the bloodhot rush of thought
        gushing out your nose

    what might have been
    settles like dust in the ion charged after
    settles like the bigboy at second base
    settles like the now dead ball
            you glimpse again through
            a cluster of concerned legs
    where it lies
    white   easy   harmless
    beyond the broken now.

9

DONNY S.

Because I was little and
lipped back at him when
he scorned my bare legs
Sissy, he hissed

he jerked a willow switch
from a weeping tree and chased me
down Gustavus Street
lashing my calves
the switch singing thin   stinging

'til I had had enough
and turned abrupt to boot him
so he doubled grunting over
then, his teeth grating like ice
on ice in deep December lakes
flailed me frenzied
while I screamed to school
arrived in snot and tears
blubbered out my tale.

You ask me now why I do not
believe in God's justice, well
they told me
Young man, served you right
my legs flayed, my pride in shreds
never kick another where it hurts
while Donny, five years my senior,
the muscles of his arms flexing,
snickered.
Some nights still
I wake cold and sobbing
my legs exposed
the day laid bare and
down the block
Donny
with that
singing tree in his hand.

THE N. BOYS

were coarse
(though I loved their sister
who sat near me in Grade Three)
and snatched me when I was
almost by and blithely counting clouds
lifted my hat and brimmed it
with winterbrown mudwater
from the pothole where they'd pissed
five minutes earlier
(flouting)
fingers dug my arms down
while the eldest jerked it
over my eyes
so I felt the cold victim rush
of shame on scalp and neck
and face
the hot scald of tears;

when, years later
their battered mother
impaled their brutish father
their mentor
I laughed, imagining
their hurt and the hot
slip of daddy's blood on their boots
when they found him flipping
on a hook
that would not recant

but I cried for their sister
who was named after a flower and
whose smile was a hopeful blossom
opening white
in all that cruel and arid land.

BROTHERS 3

Their knees on my arms
busy fingers twine and jerk my hair
while one slaps me
and one pours dry playground dirt
into my open protest.

Hatred gestates limblessly
but when it burns into the outer air
of the seized moment
it grows strange flagella
stinging tails:

Brother One on a high swing
on a near spring day
and I just aimed right
led him as you would prey
so the iceball centered
with the horse chestnut
caught him in the eye
tumbled him over
to a flat-backed landing
on concrete
where he lay and twitched
like some spent swimmer
in nemesis' sea.

Brother Two rode free
in a bicycle time
past the hiding hedge
where I crouched aflame
and I slid the pole
into his spokes
so the front wheel locked
and the bicycle bucked
him up and over RODEO!
he planted his smirk

in the rough gravel's kiss
and all the little shred wounds wept
wee wee wee all the way home.

But Brother Three learned the wind
sniffed nervously like lost sheep
reared his head, eyed furiously
would not be trapped in my guile;
let him know though
that these thirty-five years
are barely breathing
and while he no longer lives my life
I do long for him
my smile is thin and will not heal
and my teeth still
grind with grit.

SMALL HISTORIES IN THE SNOW

We wrote our small histories
in the snow with sticks
taped and patched
held together by dreamsglue

in the streets where cars dared not
all the boys like black crows flocked
to clack and whack
at the frozen eye of winter

morning 'til the big bell called us
noons after gulping scalds of soup
after 4 as the light gave out, grey
and often, softer, after dark
in the shadowland of houselights
flecked with falling clouds

each time we left we didn't
we left our laughter

          and
we left our wooden surrogates
to hold our place
we left our sticks angled
into banks, jammed and tossed
like random runes that only we
returning to the fray
like young Arthurs could extract
and interpret into action
there on that smooth
and endless stretch of road

In the Hockey Hall of Fame I sat down and wept

Foolish in a man my age, perhaps,
but Beehive Corn Syrup
Tim Horton brushcut and
Jacques Plante diving and
cards and coins and pennants
and echoes in my chest turned on some ache
so I sat down on the bench of sighs

and wept for narrow beds shared with brothers
pillowed borders down the middle and
elbows in the night if you strayed over

and I wept for simple Saturdays
in theatres with matinees and
pink elephant popcorn
cliffhangers and shouting

and I wept for Roy Rogers twin six-shooters
low on my hips and how fast I was

and for drawers and drawers of comic books read
and reread under a rain-pelted roof

and I wept for balloon tires
riding through the leaves of fall
long after dark when bonfires filled the air
and mothers called

and green apple fights

and my first cat dying

and Norma Lynn Gallagher on the back of my tricycle
with the handlebar streamers painting the day

and I wept for Roy's Confectionary
three candies for a cent and the half-dollar sack

15

Robert McKay and I bought, heavy as pirate gold
and ate in the dark of Friday films
under the prowling nose of Mrs. Lesperance

and Ella Bolander's coffee cake
still warm and sugar brown
and Mackenzies' milkshakes
served up cold and threescoop thick
by summer girls with hair in braids

and I wept for the night
I touched Rocket Richard
and found out he was only flesh

and I wept and wept for the way breath seems
on the sharp frozen river of December dawn
to just slip away, transparent, like all those years
so easily

and is gone

AFTER

Father has his feet up, the long day leaving
his muscles unfurled in the warm bath of home
and mother in the bright pool of kitchen light
finishes dishes and hums absently along
with some old tune on the radio from Owen Sound
while outside and bellyful, supper still a resonance
we've stretched the day, the month, looped garlands of
scavenged Christmas bulbs in the willow
and under them the blue, the yellow/green/and red
game goes on, we will it, to and fro
less talking now, night closing in
and muffling all, we focus on the shadowshift
among the windblown coloured layers of air

to hold it such:
my parents young
my stick raised where I shout
the ball past the goalie's glove
and evening not an ending, no
just a delayed Christmas card
hung on the rainbow of willow branches
which sway like dancers to an old love song.

FOR ME

First
tramped it workboots flat
then withstood midnight's necessary tyranny
and the indiscriminate cruelty of spray
the stifflegged silver hours beneath a distant moon

then
big hands round my ribs
You can gently in my ear as breathing
propelled me, held me blades to ice
steady as the arc of earth
on oval sunlit Saturday
until *I could*
until *I did*

then
smiled at what he had wrought
stepped off the rink to give me room

and rested

BOYS

Skunk, Scoop and Skin
Bum, Bacon and Beaker
Fender, Fergie and Frog
Hag, Herb, Case, Clarabell the Clown
and Lucky Dollar Bob
who earned his own line
when winter one summer's day
like a sneaky backhander slid
icy into his left ventricle
and took him out of the play

boys, a clatter of boys all
scatter and noise
sweaty and rough
luminous with laughter
and tough

boys, a noun nicknamed and
trailing adjectives
like breathy interjections in sharp air

boys, who care little about men
or mothers or mortgages
or math, except as it applies
to the angle of the shot

boys, in all their beauty
shout it out before they fade:
Skunk Bum Fender Hag
Scoop Bacon Frog Case
Skin Beaker Ferg Herb
Clarabell the Clown and
                    Lucky
                    Dollar
                    Bob

19

THE WAY IT SHOULD BE

No one is chosen last

because/he is youngest, smallest

because/his polio legs cannot carry him
            his chest clenches with asthma

because/weak-wristed, he cannot shoot
            fears crosschecks to the ribs
            cries too easily
            wears a new coat, a sissy coat
            has snot caked on his face

because/his eyes cross crazily

because/he lives across the tracks
            in the haze of the everburning dump
            his father gathers garbage, is the town drunk
            his family are Catholics, the only ones around
            he has cowshit clinging to his boots

no one is chosen last, that's the way it
should and must be, the choosing is fair
and decent and instant, the teams simply divide
and then rush together, shouting, as the sea.

TERRITORIAL IMPERATIVE

Clean the road
in the name of the game
in the name of Saturday off.

Create impediments for cars.
Dam the ends of the block
with galoshes coats toboggans
(younger siblings and dead dogs, if available)
so nothing motorized leaks into
the slap of feet and swish.

Only occasionally does someone
gameless and driven (doubtless forced
into early adulthood
like a Christmas amaryllis)
try the street. But
by the way our hard black eyes
bore holes in their hearts
by the whitening knuckles
on the shafts of our sticks
by the stretched silence
conspiring to arrest them
they can tell that reverse
is the only gear for them
that only in retreat can
breathing again resume
that they have unwisely
ungainly, uninvited wandered
into the inviolate imperative
where childhood rules.

Real lives

I always chose Richard, others followed
with Howe and Plante and Kelly
Hull, Delvecchio and Keon
Bower and Beliveau
names pulled from airwaves
from corn syrup tins
from crisp 5 cents packs
still sibilant of gum.

Did those heroes ever stop
in the Gardens or the Forum
in the fullness of their strength
with the crowd in their hands
and feel the faint echo
of that small town far away
in the chaos of our play
where a sponge ball spun into homemade nets
        the player's bench was carved from snow
        the teams were made/unmade by whim
        the rule was thrash and squabble and run

did they ever pause to realize
that somewhere on the edge of fame
they led dual/brighteyed/vivid/
and much more vital lives.

"FOR WHAT THEY MIGHT HAVE BEEN"

for Richard Harrison

Bobby Orr is eighteen and
so am I, is there a better age?
Toronto the Gardens front row blues
my first NHL game
we are rookies, is there a fresher thing to be?

on my way to Vancouver   a train waits at Union
long and asleep
breathing in the crisp March air
at midnight we leave to traverse the great land
eat up the width of a continent
I have never been out of Ontario, I think
the crowd raw and restless around me

and below on the bright hope number 4
takes the puck behind his own net, *Imagine,*
says my father, *you're his age*, and Orr
finesses his way all swoops and arcs
the hostile length of the ice, a meshing
of shush and glide, the puck
some marriage vow he intends to keep, tucks it
high to the glove side and
no Leaf lays a stick on him

I know now I am seeing
and for three days of trees and rocks and lakes
then prairie, the flat metallic flick of poles and poles
till mountains, gorgeous, tumble to the sea
I think, *he is the same age as me,*
and I am him, am I not, eighteen and full of grace
going end to end

IMAGINE SHE'S GOING BACK IN

to Val, for all the leavings

Two men have left behind their families, sleeping,
cocooned in body warm sheets, snugged in dreams, two
men on the clear dawn's crest move towards the game,
the white car a silent chariot drawn along the day'sridge
past the frosted fall margins, past the stunned early
graze and gaze of cattle.

From a small cabal of houses, a pause in the farms, a
cluster of dwellingshuddled, their shoulders rounded
against early winter, woodsmoke hanging like a charm
above their heads, from one such home emerges a
woman in boots and coat and long nightshirt, briefly
stops to wonder at our passage to watch us partway
along then stoops to scoop the bluebagged morning
news from the driveway   turns   and is gone.

Imagine, says Jim, *she's going back in now to that warm
house, to the kitchen where the woodstove ticks and on the
table are just baked muffins rich pats of butter amber honey
last summer's peach jam and coffee, yes hot coffee fresh
ground, swirling aromas and spiked with milk. And she looks
out, I say, out through the big picture window over the fields
beginning to glow the trees coming alive with day, the skin of
ice on the pond, maybe a hawk circling, maybe blue jays at the
feeder. And her man is there, his hair tousled sleep still in his
head, he is sitting near the stove his big brown hands cradling
his coffee savouring, and she hands him the paper over his
shoulder, he leans his head back and releases a slow smile, she
bends from above to kiss the morning from his lips.*

Suddenly the white car is thick with longing, we are now
well past this woman, this man, the contented flex of
their lives, but we cannot let it go, it's just that now we
do not talk we just silently (if we spoke it aloud it would

24

shatter our brains attuned) we just silently imagine: she
bends from above to kiss the morning from his lips and
she is beneath that velour robe that flannelette night-
gown naked, her breasts relaxed unfettered and heavy
against the cloth and still they kiss, she moves around
that rocking chair and hugs him Sunday morning wide
and long, he slides those brown hands to the pleasing
convex swell of her belly where their children slept and
grew, slept and grew, he traces the slow curves of those
years and she puts her face to the rough welcome of his
cheek near where the neck turns soft even in men and
the contented pulse sings do not move   and so they'll sit,
the window upon the day the table full awaiting their
attendance.

We drive yes we drive, into the sun towards the edge of
the earth, our eyes on the road but our minds braided
like rugs on the pine floor of that kitchen, not on the
long hour unfurling   drive still.

PACKING

Nothing must be forgotten, this must be done slowly,
carefully, purposefully:
First the towel, for when the game is over and your body
pleads for the massage of steam and water. Then the two
sweaters, the red then the white, always that order, you
don't know why just do it, it came to you in a dream like
a pass out of nowhere. Then the shin pads' long lean
parabolas, the elbow pads tucked against one another
like sleeping lovers, the gladiator helmet & cage where
your brain will prowl, the shoulder pads folded left over
right, always, the gloves, palms still soft and promising,
one at each end to add some symmetry. Next the blue
sweats, the t-shirt, the garter belt, the jock, the skate
socks, the big socks striped and ready to contain. The
pants' unwieldy armour. Then the skates, treat them
kindly, with respect, they are your friends your best
friends, they fit you and you alone like your fingerprints,
you slide them into the side pockets then as you zip

look ahead   concentrate

Think of your winger, think of being in his skin breath-
ing when he breathes, when he turns you go with him he
is yours, if each man covers his own the system works.
Think of being shorthanded, think of long minutes play-
ing the box four of you in perfect sync, keep the shooters
to the outside outside is all motion no harm keep them
from the slot keep the center clean, make them pass time,
don't even consider the other end your world has
shrunk, just kill the clock stay in that square.

Think of line changes, prepare yourself, wait, watch for
him to come off, brace your feet vault the boards hit the
ice skating get both hands on your stick, measure the
play look for your lines to appear be ready to say them
like a mantra

zip up the bag.
Now pick it up
over your right shoulder how many thousand times
have you felt the weight shift? so you are ready for the
tug then the drop steady your feet with your left hand
pick up your sticks, heft them, feel the way they nestle
into your welcoming grip, see the fresh black tape how it
wraps and overlaps smoothed so no irregularities mar
the way of the puck. Kiss your wife and children good-
bye open the door
                         step out into a winter order
into the crisp predestined clarity of your vision.

I feel responsible, I was the last one to see him (alive? is
left unspoken, no one wants to be the one to have that
word brand his lips, it shows a lack of faith, and what is
hockey, if not faith? I ask you).

3 a.m. I roll over, drugged with night, someone down
the hall is screaming *It's okay, it's okay, it'll never leave the
room, you can trust us, we're your friends.* See? Trust. Faith.
Followed by a thump, another yell, this one wordless, as
if in exorcism.

His shadow occupies the chair by the curtained window.
It is his eyes, aglow in a dark face that I see (or think I
see, because this is now fast seeming a dream, I'm not
sure I could or would swear to it). Goalies have those
eyes, late into the night eyes feverous with self flagella-
tion at that shot that trickled by, if only I'd played the
angle better, kept my stick on the ice, stayed on my feet,
anticipated, choose one, or all goalies are tortured, their
heads VCRs on endless loops that play and replay every
movement into a slow freeze.

Go to bed, it's late, big game in just a few hours. My mouth
barely working, maybe I don't say that at all, maybe I
say *What?* The face I can't quite discern responds *I will,
just let me finish this beer,* or maybe it doesn't, maybe
what I hear is in goalie talk and can't be translated. I see
a glinting tilt, hear an amber swallow, eager, and then
I'm out, even the screamers now done, all that can be
said, said, the weight of the day on them like wet sand.

Then it's day slapping me alive and the goalie is gone, I
mean completely. Suitcase, equipment bag, car. Car! he
was too drunk to walk, oh god, head-on family wiped
out toys strewn cruelly   or upside down into deep
rivers, or flattened against unyielding rock cuts, one
when still spinning the evil slish of gasoline snaking to

28

the hothot motor. The goalie is gone and a team without a goalie is no team at all. He is the crazy one, the one who chooses crucifixion, chooses the one on one the slap shot the tip the Horatio at the bridge après moi le déluge.

Out in this bright sun which tries its edge on my eyes the team has gathered to murmur, to speculate. I stand accused, it was my job to watch him, to guard the guardian when his guard was down, to save him from himself. But everybody know goaltenders are unsave-able, its their job to save. We huddle in the frost, stare at the space where his car sat, no one wants to say *forfeit* but it's there, the clock is moving the sun rising the ice waiting.

The big defenceman stirs, I've seen him calm as poetry break up a four-on-one, we all defer to him, he says *We'll go to the arena, get dressed, take the ice if necessary, I know him, he'll be there.* We all grasp this, like a stick thrown to you from the bench, your other lying shattered in the corner, the play leaving you. We as one, as the team, turn toward the game   after all, what is hockey but turning your back on the goalie and knowing, what is hockey without faith? I ask you.

Put it away

Wash what you can
the rest abandon to outside forces, the ministrations of
April let the sun with its newlyfound fingers knead and
the wind, its edges rubbed smooth, sing softly around
the blades through the eyeholes of your cage   let
robins perch where pucks did   mound the picnic
table with winter's leavings   sag the clothesline
do your sticks too, in a bed of fresh grass   even wood
needs to breathe, recall treedom

Leave it for seven days and nights
days to soak up bliss, to feel that this is right/ and
nights' ice blue and blazing skies to feed its fervent
frozen past.   Then pack it   leave the zipper open
one sigh so even in twenty weeks of long and heavy
sleep, dreamless in the darkness like perennial bulbs
strengthening it knows

Hockey is not summer nor was it ever meant to be.

Take your clue from the angles of the earth   wait
so when the September days turn and tilt and frost
begins to write invitations something in the snap of air
tells you it is time to put away the recumbent laze of
longer unfocused days.
Go then to the basement, the bag waiting with its world
within, open it to layers of sifting snow renewed, pucks
& passes, voices raised in praise fresh as the north wind.

Ask the ponds where it began: everything has its bor-
ders.

I DON'T WANT TO BE **44**

Like an errant pass for an outbreaking winger that leaps
off your stick snorting and unbridled   misses
clatters wide off the boards and down the long ice and
the linesman's hand rises sure as judgement the whistle
shrills and your teammates' heads slump as one   you
can almost hear them say through the pulse of shame in
your helmet
Screwup, won't he ever get it right?

Like a shot you can block, that you're sure that you own
your body is a wall of gristle and pad not a wish could
get through but a wish stronger than yours released
from the swish of a stick, from a taped blade down the
tapered moment, a wish frozen and black that finds a
hole (you swore you were whole) gets by leaves the
goalie gaping   t r i c k l e s
in
you thought you would stop it all you did was
Screwup, won't you ever get it right?

Like the last morning of fall all brightedged and colour-
sharp that you left to enter this winter world of play
now turned to midafternoon grey and scudding, the
horizon beginning to smear and fat wet derisive kisses
tumble slop into your long face as you lug the sodden
mass of your tired equipment across the the black park-
ing lot to your car and notice not for the first time but
more clearly now the rust beginning to eat at its margins
look up into the half snow unsure sky   think
Today I'm 43   before long   before I even get my
breath back 44
and I don't want to be   won't it ever   slow down?
long enough for me to lay a hand on its passing get a lin-
gering look at its works   learn how?
think
Today I am 43 going on
Screwup, won't I ever get it? get it? get it? Won't I ever get it
right?

31

Occasionally you must try the center route, the way most
heavily guarded   though the odds be against you
though your common sense yearns like a siren

the direct way, through the stone Sentinels, who like two
heavy hands want to applaud your failed effort   to
jam you where eyes bulge and lungs forget to breathe

the trick is surprise the trick is audacity, the thin
moment of pause, the deke   then flip ahead the puck
like a precursor and accelerate into the wouldnotdare
threading past dread looming cliff high on either side
do not glance sideways   focus, focus and forget
imagine you alone occupy that wish   small, getting
smaller

and if it works, yes

            you there in the still and open space beyond
the puck like the next stage perfectly planned the ice
pristine the sound of freedom to savour   look

look towards the goal where he waits   had you for-
gotten?   in the swell of your success   the two
fierce eyes the goalie masked and crouching

POET IN HOCKEY DRESSING ROOM

Thin-skinned
beneath the needling
I begin to shrink, the laughter
slapping hard against the edge of
my ego: *S'yore a pote, eh?*
Kinda potree d'ya write?
Words unnatural in my mouth
as ill-fitting dentures,
I apologize for who I am. I cower
like a cigar smoker who's lost his way
and wandered into a suburban health club
feel niggerish among Klansmen
    Jewish among Nazis
    homo among phobics

I am adrift in this sniggering sea.

Dumb with despair
lonely with onlyness
I dress quickly
put my other self on
stride armoured into an icy arena
where language is driven hard into the boards
where with blades and a club
my shame flying like a red flag
my tongue gone guttural
I can belong,
a man
among men.

SPIDERWOMAN

You got under my epidermis, baby

and laid your lust like eggs
    their subcutaneous fire
I can't cool this mad desire
can't ease this arachnid itch
                I'm bewitched
you have planted
          agonized delight
makes me   twitch
          in the sweat
          of the night

with dreams of hatchings
membranes taut and thin
      I wake up scratching
your name   into my skin

CHILLS RUN DOWN MY SPINE/PERSONAL

(a found poem)

You.
a beautiful creature
from the dark
skin of alabaster
flowing hair of crimson
eyes of a cat.

Me.
a kid with an attitude
and a gift for being mean.

You are an angel.
I see you so many times
every day
but I've never told you
how I feel.

YOU KNOW WHO YOU ARE!!!

THAT DAY ON THE LAWN

The Bride is the focus
the cameras seek her out
she smiles and she smiles while
the breeze loves around her. See?
her veil and train are dancing.
The throngs cluster to her
bees to her white petals
cameras click and click
she smiles and she smiles
she is white
on the green
of the lawn
she is queen
and all the guests are hers.

The Groom   peripheral
stands in the shade
a third thumb in all this applause.
Oh yes, of course
his mother plays her lips
along his smooth cheek, in passing
his sister hugs his back
before moving to the Bride
men clap his shoulder
pump his hand and squeeze his fingers
hard, as men do, testing.
But no one really notices that
he has stopped breathing.

Later, maybe aeons,
as he drinks with his buddies
during boisterous poker, perhaps
or after a morning bright with baseball
he mentions the day on the lawn
in a voice raw with regret
and the others, as one

stop laughing and turn
their damaged eyes inward
sit silently in the light grown suddenly white
wincing at the shuttersound of imagined cameras
and fingering all their scars.

In the next life

I'll be a salesman
door to door where longing leans
against screens to watch
autumn leaves clatter down.

I'll knock and when Rapunzel
lets loose her fiery yearning
I'll scramble up, hands burning, I'll say
I sell satisfaction
in both metric and imperial
whatever format your hunger needs
and I'll measure open my valise.

If your porridge is too cold
I'll make it steam
and crown it with brown sugar and cream.
If your prince has aged, gone to golf
with these lips I'll breathe life
speak ballet and good books, rub your shoulders
with myrrh as he did before love gave way
from my battered blue case Presto!
pull a baby grand, play Mood Indigo.

Up Angst Avenue and down
Depression Drive
around Crying Crescent I'll stride
announced by car alarms and baying dogs
and I'll watch for bruised hopes and eyes
behind partly closed blinds.

I'll sell satisfaction, no waiting
lifetime guaranteed
be paid my commission with blank cheques.

I'll sell by truckloads, shipsful, heartneeds
the shares in Desire Mines

will triple overnight
and oh!
the dividends they'll pay.

In the next life I will succeed
where so many
have failed.

CENTERED

he sits all day
in the porch
and listens to the goings on
learning a new way to observe
what he's always known:

that this day would arrive
at the end of travels
where he'd wait, motionless as the sun
when all worlds would come to this place
to circle in his patience
        in his silent strength
        in his grace

BEFORE ME MY FOOD

I watch him wrestle with eating
one pleasure remaining of few
in these diminishing days

his fork skitters in bare patches of plate
pieces of meat avoid him
he sometimes butters his thumb
so my mother chides him
as if he were
just now learning knives

his carpenter's hands
used to the heft of hammer
the weight of wood
stumble now
at the intricacy of serviettes
and I nearly cry to see
him gamely struggle
to unfold
the flimsy tissue
as if it held at centre
the buried answer
blue   iris blue   and bursting

TRICKLE MOVING

for the Lees

The new house is waiting, there is no hurry.
Today we will move some boxes, tomorrow chairs, or
perhaps nothing, there is no hurry.
Time is on hold while we pack and repack, repeat and
repeat, we move at the pace of breathing, the new house
empty, half asleep and windows shuttered, even its
clocks unwound, no hurry, no hurry.

So slow, our going, days are not disrupted, nights pass
without tossing, meals dream themselves full.
So slow, trickle moving, this old place barely bothers to
shrug its sloped shoulders, to listen to the murmurs of
unhurried final loving on mattresses whose headboards
lean against other walls, to notice final patter of soft-
soled children whose laughter eases out like sand
through a glass gate   goodbye.
Until the last book is gone and sunset is the rug that
warms the hardwood floors.

GEORGE

Do not slake your thirst in the clear pool
of the dragon's eye, still as it seems,
and bottomless and promising and cool,
a long slow swallow past need into dreams.

Do not eat of the fruit of her voice, a sound
plucked perfect, round and green and smooth,
from the stem of your desire, newly found,
to live on that tender fleshy succubous, untruth.

And do not linger in the chamber of her breast,
cradled and rocked and anointed with balm;
to the passing world's traffic and unrest
inured, heavy, aslumber in the arms of calm.

Leap up from this easy melody,
and raising instead your singing steel,
drive it into her dragon ways!
Onward, hero, leave behind all you feel.

WARRIORS IN HEAVEN

All is long and languid here
the only blood the slow red thrum
of pulse, unhurried, in the ear

there is no drum, no fife
no rousing skirl of pipes, no scrum
no clash of steel nor burst of bomb
no rearing wounded horses' screams
no twisted midnight clouds of dreams

just the lay-me-down of war
all trace of sallies and forays
resigning, a shrugging off of armour
and the slow drift of smokey autumn days

the banners furled, the warriors, dispersed, unravel
to whisper like eidolons, like forsaken leaves
down aimless sylvan footpaths hedged in laurel
to the endless tender singing of the doves

WORD PERFECT

to John Norton, for the idea

Gimme one of those old-fashioned poems
hammered out on
a faded ribbon

maybe raunchy with beersmell
and circled with coffee rings

or spackled with blood from a brawl
when the criticism got too close
and fists restored the equilibrium.

Not one of those clean copies
tiptapped onto some grey screen
in a windowless air
conditioned room
then run with hiss and hum
on the diffident laser.

Gimme something crumpled from
the back pocket of life.

Not something born under glass
fit only for the mortician's gloved hands
the collector's permanent gaze.

WAITING FOR A FRIEND

When a friend does not arrive
and the clock drones on
and you've thumbed through all
the used book stores
and nursed three coffees
and pissed them out
scanned very wrong face
like a country road gone
awry on a lying map

and still he does not come

the edges of the day dissolve
until there's nothing left
but you and scudding wrappers
on a corner now in shadow

SHELF LIFE/F.P. — NEAR MY FIFTIETH BIRTHDAY

The faces in my yearbook
stare back at me in black and white,
recite the long familiar litany
of pet peeves and future plans...
this one dead,
that one gone drunk,
the rest   to a wider middle

Maybe back then
before the colour flooded in
things were cleaner, kinetic,
and promises became ripe
mitosis in the hometown womb,
burst into the bright air of leaving
where they grew wings

only
to be netted
by strands as tight as mortgages and marriage vows
flapping
struggling
clipped
bound
shelved
like yearbooks:

shrugged in by wood
dreaming on beds of dust

Preparations for war/Jan. 16, 1991

The children have been put to bed,
the cats curled in the sweet tuck of their legs
hum throatily some song of sleep.
The fire has been granted new birch logs
they too sing, a sighing chimney hymn
and pass their gentle fever into the corners of the room,
even where the fish tank bubbles and the Angels hover,
even where the spider rocks in the strength of her web
and dreams fat dreams of flies.

I lock all the doors against the night, then walk
past my rows of books and let my fingers trail
along the rough beauty of their spines,
hear them whisper,
like friends, wise words, listen, *listen, listen,*
be content.

Then the lights I extinguish, for such is still my power,
and sit in the dark in the warm in the love
and say, *Let it all come down   if it will!*
I'll not budge from here if the stars themselves should fall.

SUNDAY MORNING FALLING

If there were a God
he would recline here beside me
Sunday gentle
as my children laugh and leap
leaf ecstasy full;
he would sit
grandfather still,
October blue eyes
drinking in
their giddy plunges
their headlong delight;
he would be filled by their sensation.

Down the street
greysuited people huddle
safe from the sun
in their brick temple
preach that the wages of sin is death
that the road to gold is denial of self.

God would not, on my front lawn,
have grey steel mallet hands
to pulverize transgressors' sordid heads
like wormy walnuts.   No,
he would have brown farmer's paws
smelling of humus and hay,
open and leather and warm,
where laughing children like these
could lay their heads, gaze roundfaced
into his autumn beard
at the dazzle of his grin
and he would chuckle, throaty and read,
and say to me without irony
My God, Bell, you are a lucky man!

while multi-coloured heaven falls
around us and the kids cartwheel
and he'd lean back on the crisp carpet
look through the maple limbs at the sun,
at the firmament, his firmament wheeling,
at the grand outside of all.

Satisfied, he'd close his eyes
and dream, child pure,
of lunch, pipe smoke, coming winter,
while the trees drop
          and drop
                plack
                plack
                plack
a cover for his fine fatigue,
and my children, satiate,
nest inside his arms,
sing to him, high and clear,
sing to him
that he is home.

2AM IN THE A&P

I find myself wandering, no,
make that wondering:
Just what am I doing here?

Hunger never sleeps.

The whole day is inverted;
while my laundry tumbles dry nearby
I grocery shop
in zombie land.

My eyes feel dry
just like those
of trout stretched
under plastic wrap
and I can't really inhale
this fluorescent air
and the checkout woman's face
is nightshift green, she snaps her gum like gunfire
echoes
she snaps the strap of her black bra
where it pinches her mushroom white shoulder
and gazes fondly at the midnight butcher
who grins so his silver tooth glints
who thwacks his cleaver down
                              down
                              down
                and three chickens become
six!

and the stockboy cleans something
stiff and gritty
from beneath his broken nails with a seriously large
knife
while the clock on the wall mumbles seconds away
and all the fruit that's left

51

is spoiled
the bananas mottled
the cherries chancred
the grapes soft as crushed skulls

and I wish I were where normal people dream
where the air is soft with sleep
and through the open cottage window
the mock orange weaves its heavy spell
and the hush of waves is all is all

instead:
tiles and chrome and a still empty cart
with one wheel jammed
like a stubborn fool;
in my hand a list of needs I cannot decipher;
down all those aisles my dark journey

and I ask
Who?
Who made the night
so long?

PUMPKIN PIE

I come for the punkin pie, he says,
his face bristled white with a few days growth
his one pantleg tucked up in his sock,
the other loose and crusted with mud,
to no one and everyone in the store he repeats
I come fer the punkin
there's nuthin' but razbury
left on the shelf, now what'll I do?

Existential and wailing he wanders.
We try to ignore but he sticks
and he follows, through bread and soap
and past frozen juices,
I can smell him behind me and forget to buy bagels,
hear the rasp of his breath and miss out on salmon
imported today from the deep cold Atlantic,
I come fer that pie
and I speed up my cart
through crackers and mustards and racing in fruits

then he's gone
and I see him glued to the deli,
eyeing a tub of coleslaw and turning
it over as if looking for answers
to pumpkin pies missing
and where's Jimmy Hoffa
and the other great puzzles.

The last I see of him
he's purchased sliced ham
and gripping it so it cannot escape
so its juices drip and pursue him out
one last *I come fer the punkin pie*
through doors that sigh behind him he leaves
to be swallowed
by this night's uneasy compromise.

53

MOON AND MEN

What happened has something to do with the beer
how many? lost countdown to touchdown three hours
and dropping
and the night, sweet hot
buttered with summer and melting around us
I think I was 20
going on 200
and there were three men crammed into a tin can trailer
and I was one
and six eyes bleary and beery
squeezed and squinty from the rabbit-eared snow on
a black and white twelve inch worn for worse screen
on which three men in a tin can
somewhere close overhead, I know because, see
I stumbled out the door
and reached up to touch the moon
just there
to palm her down like a silver ball
and instead fell onto the sweet grass of midnight
cause my legs had drunk way   too much
and laughed at me
so I lay there instead looking out
wondering up at a wish unfolding without me
at a mileswide black and silver swath
on which three men hovered like new horizons
and one stepped out on wobbly pins
out of the summer heat of his tincan
tinyman flyspeck in the eye of God space car

onto the dew cool surface I know
because I lay there beside him
breathing the deep blue dream
awed at his eye smile through his visor
        at the view from up here and

later: seconds: hours: may be years?
I went home and my mother said

Won't you stay up and keep watching? Son?
but how could she know I was
bent from where we'd been
and needed the susurrous of bed
like some forgetfulfilling envelope
tired drunk from where we'd been that tv'd silver'd night
and from where we still   look up   look up
had to go

THE PAPERS THAT HE BURNED

for Michele H.

Michele says that after
the stroke slid its hurt into his brain
and there set loose his losses,
her father poor father sat and cried
about the war

about la gare de Cologne
its skylight open and indecent,
about the garden long untended
and the house run to ruin,
about the children packed like panic
on the first train out
while he hung on the radio like an old suit coat
for the word no one should hear
(and no one wanted spoken)
about the papers that he burned
about the histories he annulled
to keep them from the hands
of those who would not love them

and all Michele's words could not staunch his weeping
for the wounds of his eyes were far too deep
Papa, Papa, ici il n'y a plus de guerre
but he said, as he rocked in a chair in the dark
Il y'aura toujours la guerre
ici
as he pointed to his skull
all opened by the stroke
to the papers that he burned
to the laughter extirpated
and he sobbed and he sobbed
though she stroked his crumpled brow
Il y'aura   il y'aura
toujours
la guerre.

CRABAPPLE TREE

Up where the leaves sing
with sun easy on my bare back and the sky
just becoming true fall blue

the tree is full and lazy
with apples and bees and me, we coexist
peace reigns, apples, ripe red tumble
like small thunder into my basket
bees drunken stumble, often warn me
but I am unafraid and merely sharing
and so they do not sting

the redripe wind warm beefull day reigns

later I stir the welcome juice
still it holds the eye of the sun
thicken and stir, stir and thicken
think how firm, how sweet, how lovely
the jelly then will be(e)

WALKING TO MELDRUM BAY TO A BAKESALE

I

The way to walk alone
is to set goals:

Welsh's Island first,
which isn't an island
or is
at the whim of water
and wind

Keller's Cove
where John and I
20 years past
fished for lazy
easy bass

White Seas
curious horses' greetings
and a distant dog

then Highway 540
my feet feel the difference
and my eyes explode
into full sun

the Bass Lake road
the old sawmill
then the turn into Meldrum Bay
houses tumbled up a hill
boats at rest
the end of the road
    540
    stops

if you go on
you step off
the edge of this earth

II

stopping to pee outdoors
is more satisfying
here there is no porcelain intermediary
just the glinting stream
into the earth
the grass and rocks, deep in their dream,
seem to accept

III

I see cormorants and cranes.
I hear loons.

A small green snake
pauses
to examine my shoe.
I ask its name and
its black tongue replies
in a voice too flicked
too high for hearing.

Deep burgundy butterflies
or moths
like wild fruit
edged in yellow
bob
and settle all around
sharing the late August sun.

It strikes me:
there is so much
I do not know but
then it strikes me again:
the green snake, the buttermoths
on the twisting
end of this island
have no name for me
and thus I am   and hold
no need for needing

IV

arrive at the sale ahead of time
my mouth all saliva
scouting pastries;
it starts early and I seize
a wild raspberry pie
and deep butter tarts;
there is a flurry of appetites;
a fat beekeeper from Fergus
extracts himself eagerly
from his sighing car he
buys wild grape jelly
and rumbles past baking
his girth like wild beekeeper's jelly
moans when he's told
I got the only raspberry pie
and eyes it
but the way I grip my walking stick
warns him
and he buzzes
heavily away.

V

waiting for Valerie
who is late with the car
I check
recheck
my impatient watch, grow angry   then
where I am
comfortable in the sun
the bay blue, the boats under sail
beside me, wrapped and waiting,
a tongue's treasure
I remove my offending watch:

time holds no sway
become one with the day

I'LL BE THE ONE

I'll be the one one wearing the river
a slow wrap, lazy and turbid
mud-brown and room enough
in the pockets for pike and
snapping turtles in the buttonhole.

Around my neck the blue sky scarf
held by a spray of Queen Ann's lace
and the west wind on my head
a wild hat tossing trees like bons mots.

There'll be beesnests buzzing in my smile
and grackles cackling in my hedgerow eyebrows
jackrabbits rocketing synapses in the
tawny meadows of my wheatbeld brain
wolverines on my feet for dancing
and a dusty country road for my cane.

You'll know me; even though
you're long gone, I haven't changed.

ABOUT THE AUTHOR

Roger Bell lives in Tay Township, Ontario, with his wife, Valerie, and his two daughters, Blythe and Caitlin. He teaches English at Ecole secondaire Le Caron in Penetanguishene.

His chapbook *Mythtakes* was published in 1984. He is a two-time finalist in the CBC/Tilden/Saturday Night competition.

In 1997, he was the first winner of the Shaunt Basmajian Chapbook Contest for his book Luke and the Wolf. Roger is an avid (although, by self-admission, not very talented) player with the Midland Saints hockey club, and five of his poems appeared in the hockey anthology *That Sign of Perfection.* published by Black Moss Press.